Internet checked (date) _1-8-20_ (by) _V_

Title _WWII Photo Journal_

Published (date) _1989_ # matches _3_

Compare from $ _12.90_ to $ _49.99_

Notes _____

_____

Booktique price $ _18.00_

CONSTANCE STUART LARRABEE
WW II PHOTO JOURNAL

Constance Stuart Larrabee

The National Museum of Women in the Arts
Washington, D.C.
1989

Frontispiece: D-day Beachhead, The Riviera,
France, 1944

Published on the occasion of an exhibition organized by The
National Museum of Women in the Arts and circulated by
the Smithsonian Institution Traveling Exhibition Service.

Publication supported in part by a grant from The Kent
County Arts Council.

Library of Congress Cataloging-in-Publication Data
Larrabee, Constance Stuart.
    Constance Stuart Larrabee: WW II photo journal.
    Catalogue of an exhibition at the National Museum of
Women in the Arts, Washington, D.C.
    1. World War, 1939-1945—Pictorial works—Exhibitions.
2. Larrabee, Constance Stuart—Exhibitions.
I. National Museum of Women in the Arts (U.S.)
II. Title.
D743.2.L36   1989   940.53'022'2   89-12395
ISBN 0-940979-08-X

Catalogue designed by David A. Fridberg,
MFM, Inc., Washington, D.C.

Catalogue printed by River Press, Chestertown,
Maryland

PREFACE

To commemorate the 50th anniversary of the beginning of World War II and the 150th anniversary of the camera's invention, The National Museum of Women in the Arts is proud to present a major exhibition of war photographs by Constance Stuart Larrabee. Internationally known for her documentary photography, Larrabee's work has been included in important exhibitions from Edward Steichen's *The Family of Man* (1955) to Frances Fralin's *The Indelible Image* (1985). In addition, major exhibitions of her African tribal photographs at The Corcoran Gallery of Art and the National Museum of African Art have received critical acclaim.

Constance Stuart Larrabee: WW II Photo Journal at The National Museum of Women in the Arts will introduce visitors to an important body of her work never before exhibited in the United States. These photographs record Larrabee's experiences as South Africa's first woman war correspondent in World War II. Born in England and reared in South Africa, she covered the Allied invasion of Europe for the South African magazine *Libertas*. She relied on her camera, rationed film and her wits to produce a series of photographs that documents the suffering, as well as the humanity, she witnessed during her year with the Allied armies.

I have known Constance Larrabee as an artist, friend and fellow dog lover since the 1970s. For the last thirty years she has worked not only as a photographer but as a champion breeder of Norwich and Norfolk terriers. Hanging in my office is a poster from Larrabee's exhibition *Celebration on the Chesapeake* (1982), which captures the entire sense of a dog's enjoyment of life. Her attention to the moment shines through in that picture, just as her respect for black culture is reflected in the ethnic photographs and her understanding of war and liberation is manifested in the World War II images. It is a personal honor to present Constance Stuart Larrabee's photography at the museum. A true woman of the arts, we look forward to her future work as we appreciate the excellence she has already achieved.

Anne-Imelda Marino Radice
Director

ACKNOWLEDGEMENTS

The National Museum of Women in the Arts would like to express its appreciation to Constance Stuart Larrabee, for her untiring cooperation in making this exhibition a success. Her generosity, counsel and strength of spirit, as well as her photographs and journal excerpts, have resulted in a unique show.

We would also like to acknowledge the scholarship and dedication of Susan Fisher Sterling, Associate Curator, and the editorial skills of Brett Topping, Director of Communications. The museum thanks Stephanie Stitt, Registrar; Susan Kitsoulis, Exhibition Designer; Randy Greenberg, Exhibition Assistant; and Elca Kemler, Curatorial Assistant, all of whom assisted in the design, production and installation of the show. NMWA's special appreciation goes to Kathleen Ewing for her interest in the exhibition, as well as to Jack Radcliffe and Diane Gray, who assisted Larrabee in organizing the photographic material.

Finally, we acknowledge gratefully the generous sponsorship provided by the Smithsonian Institution Traveling Exhibition Service (SITES) for the upcoming tour of *Constance Stuart Larrabee: WW II Photo Journal*, and thank the Kent County Arts Council for their important contribution to the catalogue's publication.

Constance Stuart Larrabee's World War II photographs are a visual time capsule, taking us back nearly fifty years to a world at war. Through the photographer's vision, we become enmeshed in the human drama of the liberation of Europe. Her photographs transcend the typical to reach the level of the monumental and unforgettable. They record wartime scenes, from American ships poised for battle on the Riviera coast to windows thrown open in celebration, from the shame of female collaborators to the pathos of frozen German corpses. There are a few striking images of physical brutality and social trauma; yet, overall, the photographs capture the sense of renewal and regeneration imparted by the prospect of war's end. Larrabee witnessed that brief moment of optimism and hope before the world experienced the devastating realities of the death camps and the Bomb. The jubilation of liberation, the dignity of individuals, the morality of the struggle and the human costs—these are her themes.

Constance Stuart was born in England, grew up in South Africa and studied photography in London and Munich. Her training in Germany was important. There, she shed her romantic pictorial style in favor of a straight, unmanipulated approach to black and white photography. On her return to Pretoria, South Africa, in 1936, she opened the Constance Stuart Portrait Studio, and soon earned a reputation as a fine portrait photographer. Her work was in demand by leading statesmen, generals, artists, writers and theatrical personalities.

While she achieved success in portraiture, her involvement with photography moved beyond commercialism. Working on her own and with missionaries, anthropologists and educators, she began photographing the ethnic life of South Africa. Her earliest work as a documentary photographer dates back to these strong, deep, proud portraits of vanishing black cultures. She now recalls: "I always wanted to be a photographer. I had one road to take; there were no others. Art begins with a struggle to perfect one's technique. I had no doubt that photography was an art. The camera could be used as an instrument for expression just as a painter uses his brushes."

Larrabee's reputation as an accomplished young photographer resulted in her being accredited as South Africa's first woman war correspondent in World War II. Her pass to enter the European theater in July 1944 as a representative of *Libertas* magazine stated: "One Rolleiflex camera and 18 rolls of undeveloped film were brought into this theater by Constance Stuart . . . War Correspondent for the South African Press."

Sent to Egypt for six weeks, she managed to change her orders so she could move closer to the front. In Rome she shifted course unexpectedly again, when the Allied armies began the D-day invasion of southern France on August 15, 1944. With great anticipation and excitement, she flew over the blue Mediterranean in a yellow Mae West, bound for the French Riviera. There, her personal journey truly began. For the next six months, with one small camera, this novice photojournalist moved through France with the Maquis (the Free French), the American troops of the Seventh Army, the French Army and the Royal Air Force. In the winter of 1944-45 she joined the Sixth South African Armoured Division in northern Italy. The Americans called her "Red" and the English "Ginger." The French simply called her *courageuse*.

Her uniform was as international as the armies she photographed: British boots and a paratrooper's silk scarf, an American helmet and jersey, a South African raincoat and slacks held up by a French belt. As the Allied armies pressed forward with the liberation of France, she hitched rides in trucks, amphibious jeeps, convoys, scout cars and mail planes. She slept in mobile evacuation hospital tents, press camps and requisitioned hotels. She even stayed at Maurice Chevalier's villa in Cannes.

Being a woman was sometimes an advantage, but also a liability. The British Eighth Army News, *Union Jack*, reported Stuart's arrival always engendered "pop-eyed astonishment" among the troops, who were not expecting to see a "girl" with a camera at the front. It was always easy to get a ride—recalling Claudette Colbert's classic scene in *It Happened One Night*. Like many other women war correspondents, however, Stuart was often held back from the front for several days. Billeted separately from her male colleagues, the facilities at her disposal were often less than comfortable. She accepted these difficulties as part of the war, and gained the respect of the men and women with whom she documented the liberation of Europe. As Cyril James remarked in *Union Jack*, "Constance Stuart . . . has made a fine art of getting around the fronts. She has seen more of the war than any other woman I have met."

Advancing with the troops from the Riviera beachhead, she photographed General Charles De Gaulle in Besançon. She spent days with the Maquis and, after seven weeks in the field, moved on to Paris. Newly accredited to SHAEF (Supreme Headquarters Allied Expeditionary Force), she flew over the English Channel to London, still under V-2 missile attacks. Returning to France, she rode into Belfort in a French tank, while the Germans continued to fight in the city, and entered Strasbourg in an Allied convoy under heavy shellfire on Thanksgiving Day 1944. Coming within five miles of the Rhine as the Allies were crossing into Germany, she was forced to turn back. It was her last chance to cross the Rhine before flying back to the Italian front, where she spent a grueling five weeks in the cold, snow and mud of the Apennines. She returned to South Africa in March 1945, her horizons widened and her perspective changed forever.

In 1949 Constance Stuart visited the United States and married Colonel Sterling Larrabee, whom she had met in Cairo. She became an American citizen in 1953.

Constance Stuart Larrabee's war photographs are immediate and memorable. They vividly express the best and the worst of human nature. Created under pressure, in adverse conditions, a single shot had to suffice. There was no going back, no chance to reframe or reload. Larrabee's eye is controlled and exacting, whether she is dealing with a winter landscape, a reflection in a shop window, a child with a soldier's gas mask or prisoners at gunpoint. The photographs demonstrate the beauty of her framing technique, her appreciation for detail and the unforced clarity of her compositions. Combining the intensity of straight reportage and the psychological presence of art, the works bridge the documentary and fine arts genres.

Because she was new to photojournalism and had never been to war, her eye was not jaded by sights seen once too often. She chose to photograph daily events in which any of us might have taken part. These views of individuals experiencing war and liberation underscore vital aspects of World War II rarely captured in photographs of battlefields and generals. Her images resonate with human passion and a new understanding of death and destruction. Nostalgic and genuine, they are unsentimental portraits of people, places and events. A larger context is always suggested, however—a world beyond the photograph, triggered by bits and pieces of our collective memory. The scenes encapsulate our feelings and fears about war and liberation.

Larrabee also produced a written record of her experiences as a war correspondent. Although she was not permitted to keep a diary at the front, she compiled her photographic notes and letters into a memoir named "Jeep Trek." It was published at the same time that her war photographs toured South Africa. Since then, the photographs and the journal have been integrally linked in her mind and her history. Like W. Eugene Smith's captioned photo essays in *Life* magazine or Walker Evans and James Agee's collaboration, *Let Us Now Praise Famous Men*, her text complements the photographs and adds to the visual narrative. This exhibition and catalogue reflect the powerful cooperation of words and images that is Constance Stuart Larrabee's testimony to the human drama of World War II.

Susan Fisher Sterling
Associate Curator

JULY 1944-MARCH 1945

Cairo, 1944

In flight: July 15, 1944 I am on my way to Cairo. Four weeks ago I was leading a simple, everyday life in my Pretoria studio, photographing men and women in uniform, envying them not the horrors of war but the excitement of new experiences. Then *Libertas* invited me to be their war correspondent and photograph the South African Springbok troops in Egypt. It is hard to believe that now I, too, am in uniform and on my way "up north."

Cruising at 120 mph in a DC-3 transport plane, we have landed every two or three hours in another part of Africa. Had morning tea in the dust of the Copperbelt on the Congo border. Approaching Lake Victoria we saw a group of thatched huts through the haze of bush fires, the only sign of habitation in hundreds of miles. We flew through the cold mist at 11,000 feet and came down at Juba. It was our first glimpse of the Nile. In Khartoum we experienced the heat of the tropics. The next morning we flew over the desert to Wadi Halfa and north. Suddenly the flat roofs of Cairo appeared and we landed at Heliopolis. In the plane we waited in the heat of a Flit-drenched fog before being allowed out into Egypt. I am now three and one-half days and four thousand miles from the South African veldt.

Cairo: July 19, 1944 Cairo, with its glamour, its noise, its uniforms, is fascinating. There is so much to see, the man in a fez eating next to us, shops in the bazaar, which open in the early evening, and belly dancers in the cabarets. I now know the charm of riding in a *gari* at midnight with a string of jasmine around my neck, the only sound the cries of Egyptians selling roses for a shilling that will die by morning. Today we visited the famous Mosque of Tutankhamen with its wonderful atmosphere of peace—men lying on rugs learning the Koran.

Cairo: July 20, 1944 Attended my first press conference today and met many correspondents. The routine of army life rather frightens me after the very individual life I have led. It's odd to be in uniform and to talk in capital letters, like ADPR, DGMS and GOA. Most of the South Africans have been here for three years. The war has moved on, yet Cairo still intrigues me.

Cairo: August 3, 1944 General Frank Theron wants me to go to Italy immediately. Requisitioned a bedroll, mosquito net and tin hat at Helwân. With forty pounds of extra gear, I must be getting closer to the war.

Cairo: August 10, 1944 Dined at the Mohammed Ali Club with the U.S. Military Attaché, Sterling Larrabee, and the British Consul and his wife on my last night in Cairo. Someone said: "You'll have as good a time in Cairo as in Rome—the war will be over next week anyhow." That is not my opinion. The war may be over in Egypt, but not yet in Europe. Have a feeling of impermanency now that I am moving on.

Rome: August 12, 1944 Nearly missed the plane to Italy yesterday—the transport forgot to stop for me. Flagged a taxi, but the driver did not know the way. Luckily the plane waited as I raced onto the airfield.

We stopped for tea in Malta and lunch in Bari, where the plane filled up with nurses going to Rome on leave. We flew over the Bay of Naples, its harbor filled with ships. An invasion is rumored. As we landed in Rome, the airfield was my first sight of wartime destruction. There is another rumor that Churchill and Roosevelt are expected here shortly. I was all for waiting around, but was dragged away to catch a duty bus. The correspondents are lodged in the Hotel de la Ville, at the top of the Spanish Steps.

Rome: August 13, 1944 Went to the Minerva hotel, to which the South African division is coming down in relays for two days' R and R." I shall not forget the scene in the hotel lobby, filled with dusty and exhausted men. I listened as they swapped stories about the war that we never hear at home.

Later, in the blackout, one of the officers drove me back to my hotel. A long metal stick, like a flagpole, was nailed to the front of the jeep's radiator. The captain said it was protection against ambush wires strung across roads at the front. In an open jeep traveling at fifty mph, these wires could easily decapitate someone.

Rome: August 15, 1944 The Allies have invaded southern France! I woke up to an empty hotel. There is a new front and correspondents are on the beachhead. Listening to their reports, it is hard to believe that two hours ago these men had witnessed the invasion. It is incredibly exciting and I envy them. Spent my day arranging to go to our forward press camp in Florence. There is so much red tape involved because I am a woman. They say, "You will never get near the front—not within twenty miles of it." Nobody is in a hurry to send me up.

Rome, 1944

Today we went to the unfinished stadium built by Mussolini for his victory parade. Allied soldiers were everywhere, against a backdrop of broken statues and headless horses. The inscription over the main building read: "A people of poets and artists, of heroes and saints, of thinkers and scientists, of navigators and explorers." There was no mention of war.

Rome: August 17, 1944 I am beginning to lead the life of a war correspondent, thinking only of war and news. Today we went to the unfinished stadium built by Mussolini for his victory parade. Allied soldiers were everywhere, against a backdrop of broken statues and headless horses. The inscription over the main building read: "A people of poets and artists, of heroes and saints, of thinkers and scientists, of navigators and explorers." There was no mention of war.

Rome: August 20, 1944 Jackie Martin has arrived from America, one of the few women war correspondents I have met. The hotel is crowded, so we are sharing the bridal suite. Jeep loads of drunk and sober soldiers roared past our balcony all night. Jackie told me at breakfast that tomorrow they will allow the first women correspondents onto the Riviera beachhead. I rushed down to the office of Colonel Astley, head of British Public Relations, for permission to go to France. It's the front, not Florence, for me!

The Riviera: August 21, 1944 It is D-day plus seven for the south of France. This morning we left the hotel in a jeep convoy. I am traveling with Jackie, who will be photographing Army nurses; Colonel Bernice Wilbur, who is in charge of all nurses in the Mediterranean Theater; war correspondent Rita Hume; and Bee Parker, a WAC assigned to a radio unit on the beachhead.

My most vivid impression today has been the color. We flew over the blue Mediterranean in our yellow Mae Wests. Spotted the French coast at 11:30 A.M. and landed in clouds of dust at the first army airstrip established on the Riviera—Ramatuelle. On a frantic jeep ride down the coast, we passed gray warships with silver dirigibles and pink houses looking like wedding cakes, their icing crumbling around shell holes. We saw civilians dressed in red, white and blue on bicycles and dusty German prisoners sitting by the roadside. We moved through recently liberated villages that had homemade flags waving from the windows and passed an inn with the timely name "Le Tranquille." We were stopped finally by the Maquis (Free French), who had found a German machine gun nest and needed our help.

Transferred to a truck that would take us to the Ninety-third Mobile Evacuation Field Hospital, eighteen miles from the beachhead. Looking down the dusty road in the sunshine, I saw a Maquis car flying French and American flags. A man was lying on its hood with a gun. Had the feeling of being shot in the back as we rushed past. We stopped to pick up a German cap, wondering too late if it was a booby trap. A field of crashed gliders was an amazing sight. The Germans had planted 80,000 poles in the ground to impale our downed pilots. Luckily, Allied casualties were light.

This afternoon at 5:00 P.M. we found the Ninety-third in a field eight miles from the beachhead. We could have arrived before lunch, if we had known the way, but were told the Ninety-third had moved. They are moving tomorrow. In our tin hats, we washed off the dirt and brown dust that settled on us during the afternoon's ride. Ate army rations for the first time at dinner. I am now part of the American Seventh Army.

The Riviera: August 22, 1944 The Ninety-third was the first hospital into southern France. It was brought in three days ago by the Red Cross ship *Marigold*. They had been through Anzio, and Bee Parker was shocked by my ignorance of the Anzio beachhead. Five weeks ago the war was only a series of headlines to me. Now it is a reality.

Breakfast at 7:00 A.M.—terrific struggle to pack my bedroll. Chief Nurse Mary Jane McCone and Mary Shears of the Red Cross showed me how to do it. We sat under a fig tree drinking Coca Cola and hot chocolate while the men took down the tents. After two years in the field, the nurses have learned how to make themselves comfortable.

The next camp was Brignoles. We were stopped in the jeep when three Germans came into a field and surrendered. (Sometimes they come toward you with their hands up, pull out a gun and shoot.) Colonel Currier, the hospital commander, was anxious to question them. I was the only one who spoke German, so I served as translator. They said that on D-day their unit had been surrounded by our paratroops. After hiding in the woods for a week, they came out today from hunger. A mechanic, a chemist and an architect—they were a tired, dirty, sad Wehrmacht.

Near Brignoles: August 23, 1944 Spent an almost sleepless night listening to a lone German plane wandering overhead. There were stray shots and a fire in the woods caused by shellfire. The Maquis were hunting for Germans in the hills. I am feeling extremely tired. On the radio we heard Rumania has capitulated. Washed my shirts today—American helmets make very good wash basins when the linings are taken out.

The Riviera, France, 1944

It is D-day plus seven for the south of France. . . . Spotted the French coast at 11:30 A.M. and landed in clouds of dust at the first army airstrip on the Riviera—Ramatuelle. On a frantic jeep ride down the coast, we passed gray warships with silver dirigibles. . . .

Ste. Maxime, France, 1944

The Riviera, France, 1944

Ste. Maxime, France, 1944

On the beachhead today . . . a landing barge filled with French casualties took me out to the American Red Cross hospital ship—the Marigold. *. . . The Americans go out of their way to be helpful.*

St. Tropez, France, 1944

In the afternoon we drove to the press camp, a Brignoles farmhouse. Jeeps were unloading correspondents, all exhausted. One war correspondent was shot dead yesterday in Marseille and another was almost shot down in a plane today. They think that the fighting will be over in a couple of days. Edwin Tetlow of the *London Daily Mail* said I could go with them tomorrow, but I couldn't get permission. The public relations officers were adamant about keeping women away from the front. Discouraged, I returned to the hospital at dusk. Arrived to learn that the Germans had set fire to Paris!

Aix: August 25, 1944 Went with radio correspondent Cecil Williams to Aix, birthplace of Cezanne. All the French paintings I had ever seen flashed past as we moved through the lovely landscape of sunflowers and olive trees. Wandered through the streets of Aix to the sound of a gramo phone playing "Whistle While You Work" and the "Marseillaise." We hitched a ride back to the beachhead with an FFI (French Forces of the Interior) officer. Seated between him and a man holding a tommy gun, I watched the landscape through a windscreen that wasn't there—it had been removed to make shooting easier.

Cecil told me that Léon Gaumont, pioneer of French films, lives here, so I went up to his villa to see him. His roof garden overlooks the invasion fleet. He is eighty-two. We ate grapes in his vineyard and talked as much as we were able; he spoke only French and I only English. Returned to the Beau Site and had the luxurious Riviera hotel all to myself in the middle of what must have been the height of the season in pre-war days.

Ste. Maxime: August 26, 1944 On the beachhead today. A GI in a Duck (amphibious jeep) drove me along the shore and out to sea. It is a peculiar feeling to drive off the road and into the water. We watched Ducks come ashore non stop. Later, a landing barge filled with French casualties took me out to the American Red Cross hospital ship. I watched as dirty, hot and wounded soldiers on the floor of the barge were suddenly swept up on a litter into the cleanest, coolest place in their world—the *Marigold*.

Did not know where I was going to sleep, and one of the ambulance drivers brought me to Fifty-eighth Medical Battalion headquarters. The Americans go out of their way to be helpful. Lodged in a former hotel, the Fifty-eighth is now a clearing station. Wounded soldiers are everywhere:

in rooms and hallways, on the bougainvillea-covered patio and under the trees. There is no running water. I toured the wards filled with Americans, French, Italians and Germans. One of the doctors called the Germans his "supermen." There are not many supermen among this crowd of young boys and old men.

St. Tropez: August 27, 1944 We went to St. Tropez in a battalion jeep. Saw a crowd, stopped and discovered it was D-day for seven women who had associated with the Germans. The local barber was shaving their heads. One, for moral support, wore her dark glasses. Another clutched her hair in her arms; she could not bear to part with it. They were paraded through the streets to the delight of all the children. It was my first taste of primitive reprisals, mild compared with Gestapo methods, yet very effective. The crowd cheered as I climbed onto the hood of a car to get these shots.

Near Brignoles: August 28, 1944 I returned through Toulon to the Ninety-third. The town had just been liberated and the dead were still buried beneath the rubble. The sickly smell of corpses had become a horrible reality. German warnings for mines: *"Achtung Meinen,"* marked with skull and crossbones. These and *"Verboten"* signs are everywhere.

Sisteron: August 29, 1944 Today we advanced rapidly toward Grenoble, along the route Napoleon's armies used. We are now more than 100 miles inland. Allied equipment pouring into France in one unbroken stream makes us all realize that Germany is now up against it. Arrived in Sisteron late this afternoon. An air of desolation hangs over this lovely old town, bombed by mistake. I am scared about going to Grenoble—no women correspondents have yet been allowed in.

Sisteron: August 31, 1944 Spent two days with the 364th Royal Air Force, the most forward Allied air base in France. I watched the RAF crews go out on mission after mission, sharing their tension as they waited to take off and their anxiety as they looked for their friends to return. They talk incessantly about bombing and strafing. Spitfires are fragile for flak. The pilots treat me like their sister. I know I cramp their language.

Marseille, France, 1944

Marseille, France, 1944

Although trams were running on the outskirts of Marseille, we confronted complete disorganization on the rue Canebière. Barbed wire, barricades and rubble were everywhere. . . . Our jeep was still a strange sight to many people here. Children surrounded us, asking for chewing gum.

Cannes, France, 1944

Marseille: September 1, 1944 Returned to my old friends at the Fifty-eighth Medical Battalion just in time to go with Colonel Mason to Marseille, liberated less than a week ago by General de Monsabert. The people we passed in the countryside seem bewildered after the first flush of liberation. They have had a hard time the last four years. Although trams were running on the outskirts of Marseille, we confronted complete disorganization on the rue Cane-bière. Barbed wire, barricades and rubble were everywhere. The Americans were just beginning to move in. Our jeep was still a strange sight to many people here. Children surrounded us, asking for chewing gum. It is issued with our rations, and we gave them what we had. Arrived back at midnight, dusty and tired. A hot bath is an impossibility.

Grenoble: September 4, 1944 Left the RAF in search of the press camp. We joined a French convoy on the main road. It was my first contact with the French army. I spoke no French, they spoke no English. We sang Carmen Miranda and French songs and felt at ease. Stopped for a lunch overlooking the Alps. I shared their red wine and ate what I hope was rabbit.

The Americans are in Grenoble in full force and sit in the sidewalk cafés enjoying the first large town they have struck. Found the press camp in a beautiful 16th-century chateau, littered with typewriters and correspondents' gear. Saw Douglas Warth, who showed me the car he had captured from the Germans.

Near Cannes: September 6, 1944 Douglas has had a cable from his newspaper to interview Maurice Chevalier. We drove to Cannes in search of the star. When we reached the house, his two tailors were looking after the place. They said Chevalier had left last February with his Jewish girlfriend. There is also a rumor that he has been shot by the FFI for appearing in Germany. We were invited to lunch. Cartoons and photographs of Chevalier were everywhere. Ate a delicious meal off yellow plates stamped with the design of his little straw hat.

Just after we left Chevalier's home, a car filled with Maquis crashed into us and we had to spend the night at the villa. It was marvelous to have hot bath, my first in two weeks. The bathroom was a delight: blue and gold mosaic tiles with bottles of fine perfume on the windowsill. We played Chevalier's latest records, danced the rumba barefoot all evening and forgot the war. All that was missing was our host!

Lons-le-Saunier: September 9, 1944 En route through Grenoble and Bourg we stopped in Lons-le-Saunier. American Headquarters were just moving in and it was hard to find a place to sleep. We ended up in a bleak old schoolhouse. Last night the dormitory was so cold that I put the mattress from another bed on top of my bedroll.

Douglas went on to the press camp. I stayed behind to have my film developed in a little old French studio. The photographer and his wife run the business in their home. They let me iron my shirt while they developed my films. The shop window is filled with photographs of the local Maquis heroes who have been killed by the Germans.

Besançon: September 10, 1944 Had to move on, since they wanted my billet for a general. Our mess here is in a kindergarten. It is funny to see long-legged correspondents sitting on baby chairs to eat their meals—almost like being in Wonderland, only the Mad Hatters and White Rabbits are American, French and English war correspondents.

Besançon: September 12, 1944 For the first time I visited a sector of the front held by the French. Sniping could be heard less than five hundred yards away, coming from a German roadblock. A French traitor, carrying a pick and shovel to dig his own grave, passed us on the way to the firing squad. The soldier in charge asked if we wanted to watch the execution. He changed his mind when he saw my camera. Later, we stopped to watch a scene that might have been written by de Maupassant. The key characters were two men, one girl and a motorbike. The girl was being taken away to have her head shaved. The little man sitting behind her dug a revolver into her ribs. He may have been jilted and was now getting his revenge. We heard of many such episodes.

The Germans left Langres last night. As we waited to move up the line, a scout car gave us two bottles of French champagne just liberated from a German truck. Wehrmacht was stamped across each label. The mayoress of Langres gave us fruit and fresh milk, the first I had tasted since leaving home; the first for some of the soldiers in two years. Milk is a much greater luxury than champagne.

An old Frenchman searching among the rubble of a burnt-out German tank found a helmet and some snapshots. An old woman sat outside her ruined house watching the Allies pass by. She probably had watched the Germans leave last night. Children waved homemade flags, the sun shone and

Near Besançon, France, 1944

Near Besançon, France, 1944

The Allies continue to drop supplies, including a shipment of British Tommies' boots last night. A Maquis with heavily bandaged feet brandished a pair of huge black boots under my nose. Many of them have fought almost barefoot, or in clogs or sandshoes, during the Occupation.

Besançon, France, 1944

flowers showered the tanks and cars. It was all very cheerful, but the patrol cars kept their guns trained on the woods to discourage snipers. I wanted so much to keep my head below the window. Instead I put on my helmet. The French called me *courageuse*.

Besançon: September 15, 1944 Set off this morning for Fort de Lomont, south of Belfort, newly held by the French. Visited Maquis headquarters, which still holds the front line of defense. In a motley collection of uniforms, these men run a perfect military operation. Commanded by Captain Meyer, they have spent four years organizing the underground movement that made our sweep through the south so simple. The Allies continue to drop supplies, including a shipment of British Tommies' boots last night. A Maquis with heavily bandaged feet brandished a pair of huge black boots under my nose. Many of them fought almost barefoot, or in clogs or sandshoes, during the Occupation.

At the observation post at Fort de Lomont, I looked through the periscope toward the next village, still in enemy hands. On our way back we stopped to say goodbye to the Maquis. They had captured a German tank and were busy painting the FFI sign on it. Captain Meyer removed his FFI armband and gave it to me as a souvenir of the day. I shall always value it.

Besançon: September 16, 1944 In no man's land today. Armed with maps, we aimed to get as near to Belfort as possible. We are never quite sure now from morning to night where the line is. The Germans have taken to razing villages to the ground. In the field peasants were harvesting and digging graves for their dead horses—again that horrible, sickening smell. In a river we saw the floating body of a German.

When we were driving through the American sector at Appenans, someone shouted a warning. We discovered we were heading for no man's land. We stopped and, flanked by two American soldiers, continued on foot along the road. Foxholes and shell holes scarred what yesterday were green fields. I knew we were under the eye of the enemy. The Germans must have wondered why a woman was in no man's land. I wondered, also, as I crouched in the grass along the road.

Besançon: September 23, 1944 General Charles De Gaulle came to Besançon today. The town was wild with excitement. It is the first time that the general had visited the south since its liberation. All afternoon people gathered in the square, which was decorated with flags and bunting. The press had special passes, and we were able to stand right next to the platform from which he spoke. I was impressed by his inspiring presence, although I did not understand what he said. I asked Commandant Barlone of French public relations what he thought of De Gaulle. "To me, he is God," he said.

Paris: October 1, 1944 This morning at 5:30 A.M. my French friends and I washed in the kitchen sink by candlelight. As we set off for Paris, each one hoped to find something of the city as it was four years ago. During that drive along the road, beautiful with its double row of trees, a road that had been used by many armies in many wars, it became important to me, too. The atmosphere in the car was so charged with emotion that I felt myself a *Parisienne* for the moment.

There is no hot water, no gasoline, no leather for shoes. Electricity and food also are scarce in Paris. The Hotel Scribe has been requisitioned for war correspondents. I don't know anyone in this new theater of the war. On Sunday afternoon I strolled alone down the Champs-Elysées and found it changed. Picture galleries and shop windows were decorated in the tricolor red, white and blue. There is little to buy. Holding a coin is like holding fresh air—it is made of aluminum and does not go far or buy much. The women are still chic and sophisticated. In some cases their makeup camouflages undernourishment. My French friends have just returned to the hotel. Churaqui has found his brothers, one of whom has lost an arm. Picard has found his girlfriend and Shelley her grandmother. Everyone feels the Paris of today is "*triste*."

Paris: October 2, 1944 Last night in the blackout Picard took us to Montmartre for a glimmer of Parisian night life. The Moulin Rouge was closed—there is no electricity to run it. We found an entertaining spot, a small nightclub where we watched Americans bringing the jitterbug to Paris.

London: October 16, 1944 I have been accredited to SHAEF (Supreme Headquarters Allied Expeditionary Force)! With my official papers I waited in the rain and fog for a flight to London. We took off in the afternoon, and, over the English Channel, the sun broke through the clouds.

Paris, 1944

Paris, 1944

On Sunday afternoon I strolled alone down the Champs-Elysées and found it changed. Picture galleries and shop windows were decorated in the tricolor red, white and blue. There is little to buy. . . . The women are still chic and sophisticated. In some cases their makeup camouflages undernourishment. Everyone feels the Paris of today is triste.

Paris, 1944

Last night in the blackout Picard took us to Montmartre for a glimmer of Parisian night life. . . . We found an entertaining spot, a nightclub where we watched Americans bringing the jitterbug to Paris.

Paris, 1944

Near Luxeuil-les-Bains, France, 1944

Soon I was looking down upon the neat, peaceful fields of England. Nearer to London we saw the damage caused by the German "doodlebugs."

London: October 17, 1944 I took a taxi down Regent Street. I expected people to be standing out in the street looking for V-1s and the new V-2 missiles, but these raids have become an everyday occurence for Londoners. In the blackout, after an evening with friends at the BBC, I took the tube to my army billet. Standing in the crowded car, I thought about how uprooted civilian life is here. When you wear a uniform and carry a gun, you expect your life to be disrupted, but not when you are living in your own home.

London: October 20, 1944 I rang up Noël Coward today to surprise him. He screamed "Red Mouse!" at the sound of my name, and invited me to lunch at The Ivy. Lilian Braithwaite was lunching with Helen Hayes, and half the cast of *Blithe Spirit* was at the next table. Eating oysters and jugged hare with Noël was a dramatic change from army rations at the front. During lunch, perhaps to encourage me, he said, "Always remember, the one thing in life that nevers fails you is your work."

The Women's Press Club has made me an honorary member. They were delighted to hear I have been accredited to SHAEF, which has accredited few women

Paris: November 14, 1944 Flew back to Paris and the Scribe. This evening Larry LeSueur introduced me to William Shirer, author of *Berlin Diary*. Larry has a radio in his room. He tells me that taking a woman in uniform out to dine in Paris is like taking a K ration to a banquet.

Luxeuil-les-Bains: November 19, 1944 Back to the front—to the shellfire, the rattle of machine guns, the clatter of tanks—and back to the mud. Back to the excitement of seeing how far we can go each day, how far the men have fought the night before. The Belfort gap between the Vosges and Jura Mountains is the key to the present offensive. Belfort opens the way to Alsace. The French PR office is full of correspondents, a sure sign things will happen.

We drove into the capital of Alsace-Lorraine in a blackout. I am less than a mile from the Kiel Bridge, over which the last German troops retreated two days ago. In this front-line city, there is a strict curfew. Few civilians are on the streets. Through the darkness I hear French or American voices, but mostly German. During the Occupation the High Command ordered German to be spoken and taught in the schools. *"Verboten,"* clear, bold and forbidding, was the most important word in the occupied territory.

Luxeuil-les-Bains: November 20, 1944 Today a French conducting officer drove us to Belfort, the gateway to northern Alsace. Passed razed villages and broken bridges, foxholes and shell holes, ambulances and jeeps and soldiers burying their dead. We watched men setting up guns in the rain and the mud. A big move is on.

Luxeuil-les-Bains: November 21, 1944 Several correspondents and I went up to Héricourt early this morning. It was freezing cold in the jeep and a couple of pale rays of sunshine helped warm us. At the front the Germans spotted us and began shelling. It was the first time I have been under direct fire.

Later we came to a field the war had passed over. German corpses were frozen in odd positions. The foxholes were empty, except for one, in which a young soldier had died as he struggled to get out. I was looking at dead people for the first time. I felt sad and sick as I photographed them. Discarded, unfortunate men, they were no longer gallant soldiers. The shoes had been pulled off their feet.

Luxeuil-les-Bains: November 23, 1944 Today Belfort again was under attack. In the streets we met tanks, not cars; soldiers, not civilians. Although the flags were out, there was no cheering, only the sounds of intermittent shellfire from the citadel. At French HQ a shell dropped so close it shook the windows; some had been shattered earlier this morning. A colonel took us up to a house on the front line. We kept down and peered cautiously from the window. The slightest movement would have been dangerous.

On the way back we stayed close to the walls. French troops were all around, moving in single file in search of snipers. I jumped when I saw shrapnel hit a soldier. In the middle of it all, a little girl walked by with a loaf of bread under one arm and an empty shell case under the other.

Strasbourg: November 25, 1944 I am part of the push on the Rhine. We left Belfort today in a convoy. As we came nearer to Strasbourg, we were caught up in endless lines of jeeps, trucks, tanks, big guns, supplies and men, stopping, moving and stopping. With the war all around me, it was comforting to be part of a convoy, even though

Near Héricourt, France, 1944

Later we came to a field the war had passed over. German corpses were frozen in odd positions. The foxholes were empty, except for one, in which a young soldier had died as he struggled to get out. I was looking at dead people for the first time. I felt sad and sick as I photographed them.

Near Belfort, France, 1944

Cassino, Italy, 1944

everyone was intent on his own job and I had to look after myself.

The roads were littered with signs in English, French and German: "Slow"; *"Ralentir"*; "Dangerous"; "Slippery Road"; "Mines cleared on roads and in ditches"; "Mines cleared twenty feet"; *"Achtung Meinen."* Barbed wire entanglements and tree barricades were all around. Empty shell cases and muddy tank tracks marked the surface of green fields. Cattle grazed oblivious. There was a rainbow. It was fine weather for bombing. Many planes were headed for the Rhine.

We passed ruined villages in which a few pathetic yet spirited people were patching their homes together, nailing boards, sacks and tarpaulins over windows to keep out the rain and snow. Streaming out of Strasbourg were ambulances, empty supply vehicles and truckloads of German prisoners. In the distance a fluffy streak of white smoke appeared. Strasbourg was being bombed.

Strasbourg: November 26, 1944 This morning we saw the devastation. Many of the old houses have whole sides ripped away. The cathedral is intact except for its windows; the clock has been taken out. Messerschmitts flew over and we ran for cover in a building that had been German army offices. It was in chaos. The French troops had surprised the Germans in their offices. Drawers were pulled out, books and papers tumbling out of them. Caps and uniforms were left hanging on hooks. The dregs of red wine were left in two glasses.

Strasbourg watched us from closed windows as we drove slowly down the deserted streets. This weekend I saw fewer than fifty civilians. The Alsatians, liberated after four years of German rule, have yet to lose their fear. They fear reprisals on their men and women who were forced to fight and work for the Reich. Their greatest terror is that the Germans will return. They have not seen our ceaseless convoys.

Luxeuil-les-Bains: November 27, 1944 Bill Taylor, the *Union Jack* correspondent, and I went on a last desperate dash to the Rhine. Our driver seemed unsure of the roads as we went through Altkirch. At a crossroads the MP warned that the Germans had just retaken the road ahead. We were now cut off from the direct road to Mulhouse and forced to detour. A gun flashed and soon we heard the bang of artillery. I could taste and smell the cordite from the charge. At Brigade HQ in Mulhouse, rooms were filled with maps

and men in uniform. The colonel advised us to be careful. This sector of the front changes hands from hour to hour. The French were launching a counterattack. We were forced to turn back within five miles of the Rhine.

Dijon: December 3, 1944 I waited at the dreary airfield outside Dijon for a flight to Italy. Our plane from Paris was late, so a pilot taking Seventh Army mail to Naples offered several soldiers and me a lift. I unrolled my bedroll on top of the mail and slept soundly. We flew over territory I had known so well during the first weeks of the invasion. Had tea in Marseille and the next stop was Naples.

The Mediterranean had changed color since August. Its opal monotony was broken by a spotlight of sun. The only sign of the war, as we flew down the coast of Italy, was the wing of our army plane. It was dusk when we landed. An American public relations officer found a room for me in the officers' hotel. This was my last night with the Americans during the war. From my balcony I looked beyond the rubble and across the bay to Vesuvius.

Cassino: December 5, 1944 On the road to Rome all the army signs and numbers were new to me. Here, there were warnings for malaria, which are not seen in France. It was great to be on dry, firm roads again after the last six weeks. Cassino next stop. Notices everywhere forbid you to get out of your jeep or off the road—the place is still heavily mined. I have never seen such destruction, much worse than anything in France. It is a sad memorial to war.

Rome: December 7, 1944 Broadcast to South Africa yesterday about my experiences in Strasbourg. As I read my talk, I stood shaking from head to foot with fright. Afterwards Frank Gervasi introduced me to the famous American photographer Margaret Bourke-White.

Rome: December 13, 1944 After four months I have returned to Rome and the Hotel de la Ville. In a week I have learned much about the Italian front. Nobody is encouraging me to visit the South African Division, now in the Apennines. I've been sent to photograph it, so I must get there somehow. On Sunday Rita Hume and I watched a wonderful pageant in honor of Saint Veronica at Saint Peter's. The procession, led by the Pope in gorgeous vestments of brocade, fur and lace, made its way slowly up the aisle against a backdrop of Allied uniforms.

Castiglione dei Pepoli, Italy, 1944

In Italy I have come to a static front. The Fifth Army is hampered by the isolation of mountain villages and by the mud, snow and incredible cold. . . . On the mountaintops men live in small, cold, muddy, dank dug-outs. . . . I was touched and horrified at the appalling life these soldiers lead in holes in the side of snow-covered mountains.

Castiglione dei Pepoli, Italy, 1944

Grezzana, Italy, 1944

Florence: December 15, 1944 The drive from Rome to Florence today was lovely and peaceful. We passed peasants picking olives in silver-gray groves, women leading small donkeys loaded with firewood and men hauling dark green wine bottles to market in carts pulled by Tuscan oxen. We glimpsed Lake Bolsena through gold and rust leaves. The Siena cathedral shone in the sun. We were driving along a road familiar to the Springboks, who fought their way to Florence in the summer.

In Florence we booked into the Roma, the South African officers' hotel. The small hotel orchestra plays "Lilli Marlene" as a waltz, along with tangos and foxtrots. They also know "Sarie Marais" and "Pistol Packin' Mama." Men from the South African Sixth Division, now part of the American Fifth Army, are here for a few days rest. I am again among South Africans after all my wanderings.

Castiglione dei Pepoli: December 16, 1944 I drove up into the Apennines today to photograph South Africans on the front line for the first time. We took the route over which the Sixth Division had fought. For the first time was in a jeep with chains on its wheels. Mud had taken the place of roads. Saw the spot where a tank fell 150 feet, and around the next curve a large sign "Jesus Saves" had been nailed to a tree trunk! As we followed the railway we noticed how precisely the Germans had demolished all lines, tunnels and bridges. The Italian and South African engineers already are rebuilding.

In France everything had been on the move. We fought in towns and cities, and moved swiftly through village after village. In Italy I have come to a static front. The Fifth Army is hampered by the isolation of mountain villages and by the mud, snow and incredible cold. The contrast in conditions is a shock. I am the only woman and not allowed to stay in the press camp. Instead I am billeted in a cold, dirty mess hall, part of the British field dressing station. The turquoise ceiling is painted with plump cupids.

Castiglione dei Pepoli: December 18, 1944 Major Morton took me down to the hospital. There were few patients and I was struck by the sight of a young boy in the Guards lying by himself in an empty ward. His legs have been amputated. It is hard to forget his suffering.

Grezzana: December 19, 1944 The Guards boy died last night.

We drove up to Grezzana today, the most shelled village on our front. In the jeep the colonel of the Twentieth Field Ambulance Corps told me about the evacuation of casualties. In October wounded soldiers had to be physically carried to the regimental aid post down tracks even a mule could not navigate. From there they were taken in jeeps to waiting ambulances.

Castiglione dei Pepoli: December 20, 1944 I visited the South African Sixth Division Cemetery today, where two of my friends lie buried. I slid most of the way in the mud, walking down to their plots. A padre moved past me in silence through the gray mist and mud to bury another casualty. Five Italian gravediggers and I were the only mourners at the grave side. The mud of open graves surrounded our small group. They were dug in anticipation of an attack that does not seem to be far off.

Termini: December 21, 1944 Plowed my way through two miles of mud to the regimental aid post at Termini. On the mountaintops men live in small, cold, muddy, dank dugouts. Some of them knew I was coming and had shaved in hot coffee for the occasion. In the weak sun many took the opportunity to put their blankets and clothing out to dry. Some were reinforcing the roofs of their dug-outs for the next snowfall. Others were cleaning their guns to go out on night patrol. I was touched and horrified at the appalling life these soldiers lead in holes in the side of the snow-covered mountains.

Castiglione dei Pepoli: December 23, 1944 A solitary enemy plane drones overhead. I am in bed with tonsilitis, wearing most of my clothes, an army scarf tied round my head. A pretty sight, too ill to care. The water is frozen, but I have been given a hot water bottle and an oil stove for a little warmth. The smell of oil from the stove is foul and hangs over me like a cloud. The room is full of cobwebs and the walls are damp. The windows are boarded up and barred.

This bleak village on the side of the mountain in the shadow of the Apennines seldom gets the sun.

Castiglione dei Pepoli: December 24, 1944 Christmas Eve. Everyone was wildly excited about the snow that is falling in time for Christmas. Many have never seen it before. As it falls slowly outside the window, it reminds me

Near Castiglione dei Pepoli, Italy, 1944

We are back in a dangerous sector. . . . They are clamping down on security. All civilians found wandering through the lines will be arrested and detained for questioning.

Castiglione dei Pepoli, Italy, 1944

of my student days in Munich. The snow has come to lift the soldiers out of their winter depression.

I am very tired. Terence McCaw reckons it is "operational fatigue," and that I've had it. It's true that I long for normal, everyday comforts and simple peacetime life. I must rally.

Our solitary enemy plane continues to fly overhead.

Castiglione dei Pepoli: January 5, 1945 We are back in a dangerous sector. Waiting to speak with the colonel, I hear bits of officers' conversations.

"Fresh footmarks in the snow—definitely an enemy scout."

"Let's check the mortars."

"The Germans took out four of our guards last night." They are clamping down on security. All civilians found wandering through the lines will be arrested and detained for questioning.

Grezzana: January 9, 1945 Under cover of heavy mist, we went up to the forward machine-gun post to take some photographs. Had tea in one of the billets, and every ten minutes a German shell exploded nearby. They always sound as if they are coming straight for you. We tried to take no notice. I did not like it much. Nine times out of ten the shells miss their mark. During a lull we walked down the road to meet our jeep. Our timing was good. The next moment a shell came over and destroyed a building we had just passed.

Florence: January 19, 1945 I have another cold, and Terence has persuaded me to return to Florence. On the way down a large notice near Prato warned us of typhoid. Only those with urgent business are allowed to stop there. In Florence I am sharing a room with three nurses who are on leave from the 107th. It is marvelous to sleep in a bed with sheets and to have a hot bath.

Florence: January 23, 1945 At one of the city gates an animated group of Italians held a Communist rally today. "Down with Nazism!" "Long live the Allies!" I walked through the Boboli Gardens, where refugees were sheltered during the bombardment of Florence, and now centuries-old trees are being cut down for firewood. I have lost track of the war for a moment, but not of its consequences.

The Ponte Vecchio is the only ancient bridge left standing in Florence. A Bailey bridge has replaced the one where Dante and Beatrice once stood. Houses on either side of the Ponte Vecchio were demolished by the Germans to impede the Allied advance across the Arno. The Florentines were given a choice: their houses or their bridge.

Forli: February 5, 1945 Today we came through the Apennine Pass to the Adriatic and the Eighth Army. This is the third front I have visited. It took us three hours over the Forli Pass, a perilous drive. Soon afterward the road became straight and flat. It is the first time I have been billeted in a British press camp. It runs in a most civilized way—dinner at 7:30 P.M., wine on the tables, bridge parties in the evening. This camp has no more amenities than the others, yet the atmosphere is that of an English home.

Rome: February 17, 1945 We are back in Rome. It is difficult to believe that I am really leaving the war. Instead of going from battle zone to battle zone, I am retreating back to civilian life via Rome and Cairo.

Rome: February 20, 1945 It is a routine procedure to be deloused. I was stunned to discover that I was not immune to these creatures. I *thought* my winter woolies were pricking me! Today I was painted from my neck to my feet and must return for one more treatment. I also took my clothing to the delousing center. They gave me a can of DDT and my deloused uniform.

Cairo: February 27, 1945 Yesterday at 6:30 A.M. I caught the shuttle plane to Cairo. We heard that the Prime Minister of Egypt had been assassinated and that Egypt had declared war on Germany. It has been suggested that I go to Bagdad for the Free French Legation, and also that I do a short tour of Greece to photograph Rhodesian troops. Six months ago it would have been simple to lure me across the Mediterranean. Now I have a one-track mind—back to South Africa!

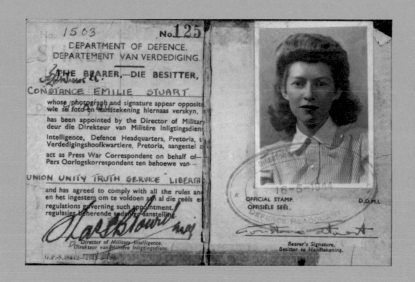

No. 1503   No. 125

DEPARTMENT OF DEFENCE.
DEPARTEMENT VAN VERDEDIGING.

THE BEARER,—DIE BESITTER,

CONSTANCE EMILIE STUART

whose photograph and signature appear opposite,
wie se foto en handtekening hiernaas verskyn,

has been appointed by the Director of Military
deur die Direkteur van Militêre Inligtingsdiens

Intelligence, Defence Headquarters, Pretoria, t
Verdedigingshoofkwartiere, Pretoria, aangestel

act as Press War Correspondent on behalf of—
Pers Oorlogskorrespondent ten behoewe van—

UNION UNITY TRUTH SERVICE LIBERTA

and has agreed to comply with all the rules and
en het ingestem om te voldoen aan al die reëls en
regulations governing such appointment.
regulasies beherende sodanige aanstelling.

Director of Military Intelligence,
Direkteur van Militêre Inligtingsdiens

O.P.S.8813—10,000 (01)

OFFICIAL STAMP.   D.O.M.I.
OFFISIÈLE SEËL.

Bearer's Signature.
Besitter se Handtekening.

No. 755

SHAEF
OVERSEAS VISA

Name MISS C. E. STUART

Licence No. 125 (SH.1503)

VALID { From 4 Oct. 1944
{ To ....

No correspondent may quit the Overseas
Theatre during the validity of this
Overseas Visa without the express
permission of the Supreme Commander.

J. Andrews Jr.   P.R.O

Date 4 Oct. 1944

(S.8813) H.Q. E.T.O., L-11,496

Miss Constance Stuart
the holder of this War Correspondents
Identification Card (U.S.) or Licence
(BR.) is a war correspondent accredited to Allied Force Headquarters
and is authorized at all times and by
all available methods, to proceed
within areas under the control of
Allied Force Headquarters in pursu-
ance of his duty of war reporting.

J. W. Clark. Col.
f Public Relations Officer
Allied Force Headquarters.

Date 20/12/1944

FSS A 3661 500 12-44

Constance Stuart Larrabee, 1945

CHECKLIST OF THE EXHIBITION

Exhibition prints are silver bromide images
made with a Rolleiflex camera and printed by Modernage, New York City

1. Cairo, 1944
2. Cairo, 1944
3. Cairo, 1944
4. Cairo, 1944
5. Cairo, 1944
6. Rome, 1944
7. Rome, 1944
8. Rome, 1944
9. The Riviera, France, 1944
10. The Riviera, France, 1944
11. The Riviera, France, 1944
12. The Riviera, France, 1944
13. St. Maximin, France, 1944
14. Ste. Maxime, France, 1944
15. Ste. Maxime, France, 1944
16. Ste. Maxime, France, 1944
17. Ste. Maxime, France, 1944
18. Ste. Maxime, France, 1944
19. Ste. Maxime, France, 1944
20. St. Tropez, France, 1944
21. St. Tropez, France, 1944
22. St. Tropez, France, 1944
23. St. Tropez, France, 1944
24. St. Tropez, France, 1944

25. St. Tropez, France, 1944
26. St. Tropez, France, 1944
27. Marseille, France, 1944
28. Marseille, France, 1944
29. Marseille, France, 1944
30. The Riviera, France, 1944
31. The Riviera, France, 1944
32. The Riviera, France, 1944
33. Cannes, France, 1944
34. Langres, France, 1944
35. Langres, France, 1944
36. Near Besançon, France, 1944
37. Near Besançon, France, 1944
38. Fort de Lomont, France, 1944
39. Near Besançon, France, 1944
40. Near Besançon, France, 1944
41. Near Besançon, France, 1944
42. Besançon, France, 1944
43. Paris, 1944
44. Paris, 1944
45. Paris, 1944
46. Paris, 1944
47. Paris, 1944
48. Paris, 1944

49. Paris, 1944
50. Near Luxeuil-les-Bains, France, 1944
51. Near Héricourt, France, 1944
52. Near Héricourt, France, 1944
53. Near Belfort, France, 1944
54. Strasbourg, France, 1944
55. Strasbourg, France, 1944
56. Strasbourg, France, 1944
57. Cassino, Italy, 1944
58. Cassino, Italy, 1944
59. Castiglione dei Pepoli, Italy, 1944
60. Castiglione dei Pepoli, Italy, 1944
61. Castiglione dei Pepoli, Italy, 1944
62. Grezzana, Italy, 1944
63. Grezzana, Italy, 1944
64. Castiglione dei Pepoli, Italy, 1944
65. Castiglione dei Pepoli, Italy, 1944
66. Near Castiglione dei Pepoli, Italy, 1944
67. Near Castiglione dei Pepoli, Italy, 1945
68. Castiglione dei Pepoli, Italy, 1945
69. Pisa, Italy, 1945
70. Florence, 1945
71. Constance Stuart Larrabee, 1944
72. Constance Stuart Larrabee, 1945

1914   Born August 7 in Cornwall, England. Three months later sailed with her family to Cape Town, South Africa. Lived on a tin mine in the northern Transvaal.

1920-   Moved to Pretoria. Given her first camera, a Kodak No. 0
1933   Box Brownie. In 1930 won First Place in Photography, "Boys and Girls Achievement Week," Pretoria Agricultural Society.

1933-   Attended the Regent Street Polytechnic School of Pho-
1935   tography, London. Apprentice in two professional portrait studios in Soho and Berkeley Square.

1935-   Advanced studies at the Bavarian State Institute for Pho-
1936   tography, Munich. Introduced to the Rolleiflex camera, which she used throughout her career.

1936-   Established the Constance Stuart Portrait Studio in Pre-
1949   toria. In 1946 opened a second studio in Johannesburg.

1937-   Began her lifelong interest in photographing South Africa's
1949   vanishing ethnic cultures: the Bushmen, Zulu, Ndebele, Lovedu, Swazi, Sotho and Transkei peoples.
        Exhibited in leading galleries in Pretoria, Johannesburg and Cape Town.

1944   Solo exhibition: *The Malay Quarter*. Opened by Noël Coward in Pretoria. Traveled to Cape Town.

1944-   Appointed by the director of South African Military Intel-
1945   ligence as South Africa's first woman war correspondent on behalf of *Libertas* magazine. Served in Egypt, Italy, France and England. Attached to the American Seventh Army in France, and accredited to SHAEF, Supreme Headquarters Allied Expeditionary Force. In Italy she was attached to the South African Sixth Armoured Division, under the command of the American Fifth Army, and the British Eighth Army.

1945-   Solo exhibition: *A Tribute to the South African Sixth Di-
1946   vision and the United States Seventh Army*. Traveled throughout South Africa.
        Published "Jeep Trek" in *Spotlight* magazine.

1947   Solo exhibition: *The Lovedu*, Pretoria.
        Official photographer for the Royal Visit to the three British Protectorates of Basutoland, Swaziland and Bechuanaland. Kalahari Desert expedition to photograph the Bushmen.

1948   Produced portfolio of photographs on the author Alan Paton and his book, *Cry the Beloved Country*. Photographs published in: *Bantu Prophets in South Africa* by Bengt Sundkler (London: Camelot Press, 1948).

1949   Married Sterling Loop Larrabee of Warrenton, Virginia, U.S. Military Attaché to South Africa, Yugoslavia (government in exile) and Greece during World War II.

1950   Moved to a historic, waterfront farm near Chestertown, Maryland. Began breeding champion Norwich and Norfolk terriers.

1952   Photographs published in: *The Basuto* by Hugh Ashton (London: Oxford University Press, 1952).

1953   Solo exhibition: *Tribal Women of South Africa*, The American Museum of Natural History, New York. Traveled in the United States and Canada through 1957.
        Became an American citizen.

1955   Group exhibition: *The Family of Man*, Museum of Modern Art, New York. Traveled nationally and internationally.

1959   Solo exhibition: *The Silent Harmony of Hand and Mind*, the story of Steuben crystal, the Commercial Museum, Philadelphia. Traveled nationally.

1979   Solo exhibition: *Photographs by Constance Stuart Larrabee*, a retrospective, the South African National Gallery, Cape Town. First solo show by a woman photographer at the National Gallery. Traveled to the Johannesburg Art Gallery and the Pretoria Art Museum as the first photographic exhibition in each museum.

1982   Solo exhibition: *Celebration on the Chesapeake*, Washington College, Chestertown, Maryland. In honor of the college's bicentennial. Traveled within Maryland and to Philadelphia.

1983   Catalogue: *Celebration on the Chesapeake*, published by King's Prevention Press and supported in part by a grant from the Kent County Arts Council.
        Solo exhibitions: *The Constance Stuart Larrabee Celebration, 1933-1983*, The South African Association of Arts, Pretoria, and The Art Gallery, University of Stellenbosch, South Africa. *Nagmaal 1947*, The Photo Gallery, The Market Theatre Foundation, Johannesburg.

1983-   Founded Washington College Friends of the Arts, Ches-
1984   tertown, Maryland.

1984   Solo exhibition: *Tribal Photographs*, The Corcoran Gallery of Art, Washington, D.C. Traveled to the Santa Fe Center for Photography, Santa Fe, New Mexico.

1985   Group exhibition: *The Indelible Image: Photographs of War, 1864 to the Present*, The Corcoran Gallery of Art, Washington, D.C. Traveled to The Grey Art Gallery, New York University, New York, and The Rice Museum, Houston, Texas. Catalogue.
        Solo exhibition: *Go Well My Child*, in collaboration with Alan Paton, The National Museum of African Art, Smithsonian Institution, Washington, D.C. Photographs now in the permanent collection of The National Museum of African Art. Catalogue.

1986   Group exhibition: *Bon Voyage*, The Cooper-Hewitt Museum, Smithsonian Institution, New York.
        Honorary degree of Doctor of Arts from Washington College, Chestertown, Maryland.

1987   Solo exhibition: *Seek What Is True*, in collaboration with Alan Paton, Duke University Museum of Art, Durham, North Carolina.

1988   Solo exhibitions: *African Profile*, Bayly Art Museum, University of Virginia, Charlottesville, Virginia.
        Seek What Is True, Mead Art Museum, Amherst College, Amherst, Massachusetts.

1989   Chairman, Washington College Friends of the Arts, Chestertown, Maryland.
        Endowed the Constance Stuart Larrabee Creative Arts Center, Washington College, Chestertown, Maryland.